Aviaries

Aviaries

Yvonne C. Murphy

Poetry Series #14

CAROLINA WREN PRESS
Durham, North Carolina

Series Editor: Andrea Selch

Design: Lesley Landis Designs
Cover Image: "Paper Garden" © 2010 Clive Hicks-Jenkins
Line Drawings: © 2010 Clive Hicks-Jenkins
Author Photograph: Stacy Karlis

*The mission of Carolina Wren Press is to seek out, nurture and
promote literary work by new and underrepresented writers,
including women and writers of color.*

Carolina Wren Press is a 501(c)3 non-profit organization supported
in part by grants and generous individual donors. In addition, we
gratefully acknowledge the ongoing support of Carolina Wren
Press's activities made possible through gifts to the Durham Arts
Council's United Arts Fund.

Library of Congress Cataloguing-in-Publication Data

Murphy, Yvonne C., 1968-
Aviaries / by Yvonne C. Murphy
    p. cm. -- (Poetry series ; #14)
Winner of the 2010 Carolina Wren Press Poetry Prize, selected by
Minnie Bruce Pratt.
ISBN 978-0-932112-63-7
I. Title. II. Series.

PS3613.U756A95 2011
811'.6--dc22

2010040540

ACKNOWLEDGEMENTS

These poems appeared previously, often in different versions, in the following magazines and anthologies:

"Skunk Lady," *Black Warrior Review.*

"Near Uvalde, TX" *BORDERLANDS: Texas Poetry Review.*

"Parrot Music Box," "Late At Night, Knitting," *Calabash.*

"Foucault's Dream," *CV2: Contemporary Verse 2.*

"Wonder Wheel," "Tijuana and South," *E: The Emily Dickinson Award Anthology.*

"Sad Mona," "Mona Rides," "Mona Thinks of Crying," *EPOCH.*

"Going to Laredo," *Gulf Coast.*

"Rest Stop, Adrian TX" *Literal Latté.*

"Autogenic," *Many Mountains Moving.*

"City Lions," "Indigo, Brooklyn," *Mobius: The Poetry Magazine.*

"The Pigeon Feeders," *Oberon.*

"Nests," *Painted Bride Quarterly.*

"Brooklyn Tropicale," "Mona Lisa," "After Hours," "Scat, Mona, Scat!" *Passages North.*

"Hummingbirds," *POETRY.*

"Late Summer," *The Portland Review.*

"Cornell's Dream," *The Schuykill Valley Journal.*

"Avenue of the Strongest," *Slipstream.*

"The Cyclone," *South Dakota Review.* Anthologized in *I Speak of the City: Poems of New York,* Stephen Wolf, ed. New York: Columbia University Press, 2007.

"Prisoner," *Stone Canoe.*

"Landscape With Birds," "The Gates," "Jefferson's Parrots," *Studio.*

"The Hirsute Woman," "Monk Parrot," *The Reading Room.*

"The Combine," "Untangling Jewelry," "The Unisphere," "String of Pearls," *The Recorder.*

"Bridge, Circle," *Redivider.*

"Girls Jumping On Beds," anthologized in *White Ink: Poems on Mothers and Motherhood,* Rishma Dunlop, ed. Toronto: Demeter Press, 2007.

"The Mangrove," *Zone 3.*

Table of Contents

I.

The Cyclone / 1

Hummingbirds / 2

The Pigeon Feeders / 3

Jefferson's Parrots / 4

Mona Lisa / 5

Bridge, Circle / 6

Landscape With Birds / 7

Cornell's Dream / 8

Foucault's Dream / 9

Sad Mona / 10

The Mangrove / 11

Indigo, Brooklyn / 12

Monk Parrot / 13

Parrot Music Box / 14

Summer Storm / 15

Nests / 16

Avenue of the Strongest / 17

II.

Mona Lisa / 21

The Hirsute Woman / 22

Skunk Lady / 24

Girls Jumping On Beds / 25

Late Summer / 26

Offering, Rio Grande / 27

Enemies / 28

Bluethroat / 29

Late at Night, Knitting / 30

Brooklyn Tropicale / 31

The Elephants / 32

Mona Thinks of Crying / 33

Mona Lisa and the Dragonfly / 34

Lost One / 35

The Unisphere / 36

Mona's Box / 38

Untangling Jewelry / 39

Prisoner / 40

String of Pearls / 41

The Combine / 43

III.

Scat Mona, Scat! / 47

Mona Rides / 48

Autogenic / 49

A Dentist's Lament / 50

Avec Kafka / 51

Going to Laredo / 52

Magnolias, Poolside / 53

Rest Stop, Adrian TX / 54

Parrot Stand / 55

Near Uvalde, TX / 56

Tijuana and South / 57

Jean Claude and Christo's *The Gates* / 59

City Lions / 60

Dervishes / 61

Housebird Suite / 62

On Park Row by the Brooklyn Bridge / 63

After Hours / 64

Wonder Wheel / 65

I.

The Cyclone

*Marianne was fond of roller coasters; a fearless rider, she
preferred to sit in the front seat.*
        —Elizabeth Bishop, "Efforts of Affection"

Nautilus of wood and steel—tracks twisted
into an exoskeleton of spirals. World famous,
"Faster than Ever," the Cyclone drops
and turns, speeds reaching sixty miles per hour.
Charles Lindbergh said it was "scarier than flying
the Atlantic solo," but Miss Moore, our poet-hero,
prefers the front seat. Her hands grip the safety bar,
waiting for the first drop *as if they knew love
is the only fortress strong enough to trust to...*

The sailors in the car behind her punch and jab
each other, tug brass buttons in anticipation.
"Surf's up," seagulls cry between dives for hot dog
scraps scattered under benches. Marianne isn't looking back,
the loop-di-loops fling her forward, catapulting gusto.
The Dreamland flea market glitters with sun, circus
freaks dangle charms to gawkers, screams from the coaster
weave in and out through tight layers of day.

Deliberate structure supporting chaos, thrills engineered
to appear spontaneous. Marianne is in her element—
the sailors gasp as her hair-clips pop out into their laps.
The celebrated braid swings wild in the air. On the ground,
Kewpie dolls pucker while boys throw balls at bottles
arranged in towers. Marianne's hair dances its own miracle.
This is mortality, she sighs, *this is eternity...*

Hummingbirds

We do the dearest, small darling
movements around and near each other.

Reverse and forward, the stirring
rush buzz of your wings.

Red, the throat full of warmth
or embarrassment as we flit

and somersault—chirping and chattering

until our bodies are together
and hover. The nectar, sugar-water

we gorge ourselves with: red flowery
feeders, Enchantment Lilies, Honeysuckle.

How summer it is with you, is with
you now, before sundown, my rareness,

my kin. Jack rabbits scurry
around the perimeter of the yard—

the mountainous backdrop of the world
immune to our ministrations.

The Pigeon Feeders

Federoff Triangle, Queens NY

They gather here. Watching pigeons scoop down for food,
senior citizens hold plastic bags with crumbs saved up
from plenty of meals alone. The aged, soft glow of streetlights
at early evening when the cars thin out on the boulevard
circumnavigates park benches, illuminating gray and white
hair. The way they come back each night, chatting a dim
clamor of gossip, sacred words about who forgot what,
who moved, what happened in the morning, other news.
Across the street, the Bagel Star gleams, a constant stream
of customers files in for lox and schmears. Pigeons sweep overhead,
then back, settling again for more crumbs underneath the trees.
One man in a wheelchair rubs his hands and rests them on his knees.
His aide talks into her cell phone, not noticing the congregation
scrambling at his feet. A metal walker stands triumphant at the curb,
a monumental H. Heroic and hearty, birds take communion
from old folks while citizens hurry to make their deadlines home.
Families waiting for their missing links—Mom, lover, or Dad
weighted down with briefcases of blessings. Busy and alive,
triangulating the sharp corners of time, physical decline.
Isn't this life's spectacle? Grieving happens in modest but
delectable moments, wrapped in curlicues of jokes and complaints.
Sarcasm and chatter blossom into flights of grace, zingers lobbed
and flung with such elegance the pigeons look up from their scraps.

Jefferson's Parrots

In his semi-circle of a room, half-moon off the parlor, Jefferson sits
writing letters to friends. It is late, the candles have dripped over

and dribbled beyond themselves, his reading wheel, strapped-new
with four books, rocks anxious in the breeze that trembles

through the door. Behind his desk, the daybed is rumpled.
Hours of reading, writing, the moon gets full waiting for his muse

to come inside. Wedged between windows and bookcases,
the door looks like it could be a window, that's the genius of the design

brought back from France, along with wine and countless *objets:*
the hand-colored engravings and china plates with painted parrots that

line his walls. *Les Perroquets,* their scarlet and indigo wings, so exotic.
He fumbles with a quill, frustrated: *Will she ever come?*

and looks out to his gardens. The night is encrusted with stars,
fragrant lavender drifting up the hill through his curtains. He wants

to will her to come, but logic overrides feeling. He must occupy his mind—
control desire, coil it up, packed tight in a snuffbox for reserve.

His head falls exhausted on the desk. The country's policies and progress
weave themselves into sleep. And the parrots bear witness while he dreams.

Mona Lisa

It's a mistake, this mystique.

A technique of thin glazes,
I look like I'm thinking.

He used urine as
a base for me
(I won't tell you whose).

He also used arsenic—
built-in bomb.

He thought he was a god,
he could have been more generous.

These hands in my lap, perpetual,
I want a pet.

I want a dog
like the other girl got.

Fuck, I hate the Louvre
(pardon my French).

Did I tell you everyone wants me?
Enigma, *c'est moi*.

All day the tourists—

I'm a girl forgotten
by her womanly body.

My robe is heavy, I need a nap.

Bridge, Circle

The Eiffel Tower was not an innovation, *a dead thing, lifeless,* Ferris knew better,
to take a bridge and twist it on its center, a circle hung on an axle, revolving,
chief sensation of The Chicago World's Fair. They thought he was crazy, a genius—
drawn from a chophouse napkin, his mighty bicycle wheel, calculated to support,
riders wondered if prairie wind would blow it all down.

Climbing steadily upwards, passengers cheered the possible danger,
growing accustomed to its novelty, the slow throb of pinions, popinjays
gasping at the panorama. His mystery saved the fair from bankruptcy, pleased
expectancy, model of efficiency, horizontal whirligig, the incredible charm
possessed by a vast body in motion—people surrounded it, perpetual, transfixed.

Ferris's wife sipped champagne on her maiden voyage, toasted her clever
husband, her gold-trimmed gown grown flush with flickers of color.
He couldn't have predicted it would be blown up later, left in pieces under
the Mississippi River—alone in a Pittsburgh hotel room, his oversized invention
could not save him, he became another bridge suspended, turned in on itself.

Landscape With Birds

...in looking at some apparently small object,
one feels the swirl of great events.
—William Carlos Williams on the poetry of Marianne Moore

The rutted field holds treasure in its grooves, every day
before Spring, crows pack into the hedgerows like balcony seats,
watching, applauding my search. Golf balls, pendants, bent
forks and spoons, metal bits of machines, fragments from bottles,
windshields, watch parts.

Corvus brachyrhynchos, the American crow, all black,
gleaming purple, onyx, smoky pearl in the sunlight.
How they rise from the edge of the field in their tri-corn hats
and black capes, keepers of wise counsel, countersinging:
omissions are not accidents, with their harsh rattles and caws.

Picking and choosing, I gather marbles, rusted cans, old keys,
chips of porcelain, combs, nails, pebbles in the bright white sun.
Before planting, I pluck accumulations from the soil—takings
in my pockets, cache of seeds, insects, broken eggshells and shotgun
casings, a dead mouse molting with a layer of fuzz, the mimicry of crows.

I half-expect Miss Moore, Celtic Morrigan, Phantom Queen to rise
out of the furrows, appearing as a hooded crow, Goddess of Regeneration,
shape-shifter poised to devour, her battle signs reflected on the glossy
backs of birds as I forage, plunder, alert to my fate, this constant
discernment with *love's extraordinary-ordinary stubbornness.*

Cornell's Dream

What a blessed benediction, what a pure joy this kind of thing
that happens with the boxes.
—Joseph Cornell, diary entry, April 11, 1957

is a series of boxes opening and closing in kaleidoscopic vision,
the ritual surprise of bubbles takes shape from a pipe, glossy

cargoes of stars float on the tips of waves. Professor Einstein
praises them, hop-skips through Cassiopeia and shimmies down

the backbone of a shell. "Joseph, my love," he crows, "you have
not wasted your time," and quotes Emily: *For Beauty is Infinity* —

butterflies balanced on the brink of a cup, chocolate wrappers,
constellations, eternity etched on the surface of a thread.

His Parrot Music Box plays *Centuries of Blue,* a do-si-do fabulation,
while Barbie dolls swing their torsos to orchestral flourishes of light.

Peninsulas and palaces furnished with glittery sand:
these playful geographies ebb out and come back home again.

To be dependent on everything else is one theory of relativity,
we must live in constant relationship all the time.

Even escape leaves us perched in cages of cut-up
newspaper margins, ticket stubs, relics of brown paper bags.

Foucault's Dream

The page of a book is not to be trusted—when opened, a flock
of language gathers to unfold and circle around itself.

We don't think that the words will take off, get lost,
disappear without any pattern or discernible trace.

No "missing" or "reward" posters linger in shopping malls
advertising the loss of a phrase, the general collapse of meaning.

Discourse is not life after all—or is it?

In his dream, he can't pin down the text,
letters become blurry birds rising from a field.

He tries to pretend that he can read them, mouths
their migrations, but the words disperse

into squiggles coasting off the page—the book is empty now,
a used-up box thrown in dumpsters at the supermarket,

its boundaries have collapsed and its calm universe has entered into fusion,
letters commingle in ways only alphabets can understand.

This was Foucault's constant nightmare: a scattering so final
it deconstructs the dream.

Sad Mona

She wonders if the background
is seeping into her.

The muddy trees, ravines she's never
seen but knows: they're there.

Mud and mud, she wonders how she feels.

Do I feel? The question is answered, marked,
buried behind her in the dingy

brown—the fadedness
she can sense in her hands, folded.

If she were lying down she would
be prostrate with grief,

a wasted beauty no one wants to know.

And would it matter if he,
if someone, came up and touched?

Would it convince the trees
to stop their noise?

Vague undertones of opera,
it's bringing her to her knees.

The Mangrove*

With a debt to Elizabeth Bishop's "The Man-Moth."

We cannot tell the rate at which we travel backwards,
underground the subways have stopped running—
global warming, storm surge, something
about squandering, rupture of sense. The planet
submerged, relics of architecture skirted by currents,
bloated structures, swimming out-of-place.

The mangroves grow through holes in drainpipes,
manholes steaming green from underneath the streets.
On subway platforms, piles of calcified trash make reefs,
congeries of vents and grates, ceramic tiles mossed underneath.
A grime cathedral—oxidized steel bedizened by barnacles,
coral accumulations, eccentric minnows darting over rails.

No echoes of the subway cars' throttle and scrape,
hurling from Delancey to East Broadway, no pedestrians
holding coffee in decaled cups. Even the violinists
have escaped, their cases scattered like coins.
The discarded cardboard of breakdancing boys flips
and spins, adrift now in stagnant water, obscured by waste.

Each tunnel curves into darkness. Dissipating
wave energy, mangroves climb toward the moonlight.
Ultra-filtrating, excluding metals and sodium,
their stalks coated with salt crystals that shimmer at night.
Dispersing viviparous seeds, propagules stay dormant
for years.

Humans extinct but for this spindrift of DNA, a propagule
floating, looking to take root. Estuarial assemblages
of lenticels, "breathing-tubes." The mangal perpetuates,
propping itself above watery trenches of the subway.
Impermeable sediments collect in protected areas, the world
could begin again, filtered, *pure enough to drink.*

Indigo, Brooklyn

Our bus runs by windows, cold blue
night: rivulets of ice cling
to each shutter, then drop off
in 3/4 time as we move
to where the neighborhood worsens.

Shadow families improvise
in front rooms lit by TV
I can't help but see
darkness nuzzled
in licks of blue light,
mutable buzzes along the landlord's
fluorescent circle, twenty-two watts,
cheapest in town.

It's a Coney Island tune,
broken roller coasters whistling in January,
Mood Indigo at the end of Sargasso alleys
blowing with papers and soda cans,
a contralto where the bus stops at a sign
and all passengers are relieved to be inside.

Steam rises in grace notes from our breath,
clouding the windows. I wipe the layer away,
glove touches glass, buildings crumble as we pass.

Ghosts of summer dart just out of sight—
how our hearts murmur for a rush of soft air!
But here, we stick to the metronome of our blues.

Monk Parrot

In a tree, over the carport, in this section
of my neighborhood there is fabled to be a bird,

a slight tropical cockatiel, hooded, cloistered last of its kind.
Monk parrot, parody on words, rhythm-a-ning in

the wings of my parking spot,
seldom seen by regular neighbors.

I call to him: *Daba deep da ba dabap.*

Our cavorting gets lost when nobody hears it,
plotted pre-planed patterns of taking off.

Sui generis jazz legend invisible to the naked eye,
we might rival the immortals if only he'd show.

A parrot response: *Well You Needn't,* over and over again.

Choruses of Benedictine brothers, birds all, join in.
Outside my window they dovetail chants among magpies,

grackles, magnificent plumage tucked inside robes.
I want the parrot to pop up where I keep watch.

Eyeing him, I'll posit: *Why not be known?*

Parrot Music Box

for Jacquelyn

Inside the pet store window two parrots perform, unpredictable
bobbles bring *ooohs* and *ahhhs* from spectators outside.

Lovebirds come in all colors—frontal red bands, yellow
under-parts washed through with orange, ruby cheek patches,

an olive-green rump, tail feathers patterned by pink,
rich gold flecked with deep blue or black.

Their bodies sit poised on strings knotted
with beads, bells, mirrors and hoops.

We presume they must be cousins, no matter
how many times removed. They coo, trilling

like flutes, feathers dazzled with sound.
We want Mozart or *Yankee Doodle Dandy*,

but from nowhere, they warble a working woman's lament:
Ella trabaja sola, solo trabaja, y su trabaja es ajeno…

The parrots pose with their beaks locked, skyward, in a kiss.
Spinning into their own idiosyncratic riffs: *kwink*

quaw, kraar, caark, kweek, chissik, fweep-fweep.
We do not know how to make sense of it, cadences

mixed of melody and noise. Brio in one language comes
out brash in another, untranslatable commotion.

The birds look out, dead-eye, through the glass—
we want them to mimic us, say: *Pretty girl, Pretty girl.*

Summer Storm

Vienna

Civilians run for cover behind Doric columns,
in the *Volksgarten*, the *Kaffehaus* empties quickly—
tourists, cyclists, coeds studying for exams
with their pens and notebooks full of urgent loops.
We crowd inside the Theseus Temple, 1820's
Athens replica. Across the park Hofburg horses
perform perfectly indoors, two students shield
their notes from torrents, cram for *The Sixties:*
Woodstock, counterculture, quizzing each other
about Ginsburg, Hippies, Summer of Love.
It's ancient history, their backpacks stashed with iPods,
videos of loved ones sequestered inside phones.
The rain gets so wild even pigeons can't fly into it,
they cluster in cornices searching for Ariadne's thread.
Huddled in narrow aisles of the temple, we must
wait it out together: *Wasser* and more *Wasser*
pools under stone entablatures, hail floods the plaza.
Friends text each other, the group gets bigger, tighter, a *Polis*.
Laments spew in various languages until everything
is swarm, alarms blaring on the *Strasse*.

Nests

Queens, NY

I can't get settled, the floor scattered with boxes,
each day filled with unpacking, placing and building.
Pigeons shuffle on the fire escape or sleep with heads tucked
into iridescent necks, pacing on the windowsills, gray
bodies anchored by pinkish feet. *Zut, zut*—nests plastered
with shit, feathers and dirt, flu and virus levitate on wings.

All day the demolition of single-family houses, wrecking
balls make way for condos outside my third-story window.
The boarding up of yards before each building's collapse,
piece after piece comes down: old refrigerators, bathtubs
idling at the curb. Each room an empty case exposed
through cracks in graffittied plywood—bedrooms,
skeletons of plumbing, brick façades torn away, tarpapered,
once stately before the long boring into the ground.

The pigeons mock me, this family of five, their burbles,
eyelids fastened to blot out the day, always coming back
to rebuild in layers of twigs and crap, imbrications of filth
flaked through windowscreens. Pest species, opportunists
surveilling from the sides of their heads. I ruined their nest
with the end of a broom, watched it crumble,
disassembled on the grass below.

Avenue of the Strongest

I can sometimes almost read the inscriptions on brick walls, in doorways,
between the wing blades of pigeons, written in the tiniest script,

the meanings of our lives. All events, every minute and detail is named there.
They dwell in circles dizzy around my window as I watch our street

called Worth where I have followed you against my stubborn will. Outside,
sanitation workers lift and haul the city's garbage tied into green and black bags.

Their headquarters roosts like the hall of superheroes a few blocks down.
Mourning doves coo at our sills: *How did we get here?*

I could not have thought to braid myself close with you. The weaving seemed
an imposition, then—strands that flattened out on top, making each other manageable.

But there is quiet peace in functioning, as we aspire from day to day.
There is hope in morning coffee makers set up the night before,

dripping their contents at dawn in faithful common time
as television reveals news of wars and famine.

We try to mellow it with milk, eyes groggy from work's long week.
There's nothing momentous about these moments, the cats curl and uncurl

to punctuate in their way. *Are we strong?*
The mesh of our lives becomes something we no longer control.

The unknowing of this certainty grows long and spindly like our fears,
our fights, our piled-up lists of aggravations. Each morning,

I imagine the garbage men take them with their load, lifting them up
with the transience of the world.

II.

Mona Lisa

It's too much.

All day, watching camera-eyed
tourists. Their bumbling
conversations (as if she didn't
understand) discerning her
as whore.

Bored whore, she thinks—
this glass box
their only protection, the only thing
keeping her back.

Are they blind?

She has no legs to get between.

The Hirsute Woman

A love story, really,
which my lover refused
to see, taking control,

he changed the channel past her
to a game, but I pleaded,
grabbed the remote,

turned back to the woman.
I didn't catch her name—
her face, an ape's, nuzzled

in the neck of a man. Her man,
who said she was his joy,
met her at a carnival

one night and knew.
My man found her
detestable, screwed-up

his face—wouldn't look,
then looked, then could only
look away. He snatched

the control and switched her
safely off. The furry-
cheeked lover, living

in Florida, or somewhere.
I imagined them always
together, naked in bed,

his arms twined around
hers, both heads finding comfort
in a sensuous carpet of hair.

Combs and brushes rested
on their table—left over
from the giddiness of flirting.

When my protest grew
unbearable, my lover finally
left the room. I turned her

back on, decades had passed.
Her husband dead now, the woman
sat somber, clean-shaven, shorn.

Skunk Lady

Combs soaked in Barbicide
told no secrets,
at Edie's Cut-n-Curl:
women lined up to be pretty.
Smiling through perm-
smell, hair spray,
Mother and I went together—
a narrow hallway bordered
by mirrors, Christmas lights
and swivel-back chairs.
Edie greeted us,
her jet-black hair
white-striped down the middle.
Solicitous with scissors,
she let us talk. At ten,
I coined her nickname,
already impatient for my own
hair to be wild. Though logic
told me I would never be beautiful,
it was important to pretend. Mother
peering into the mirror,
I practiced style tips
for the playback at home.
I did not tell Edie this
but often, on the way home,
I wanted to disappear.
I wanted to dissolve
into the passenger's seat,
a kind of vinyl light
permeating everything
like the smell my father said
was a sign of good luck,
the smell of skunk.

Girls Jumping On Beds

Mick Jagger's tongue in their ears,
real boys in the next building, drinking and dancing
and the Sixties stretched out like a caftan,
their paisley bandanas and cut-off shorts flap
as guitar solos conjure dreams of sex before husbands
and birth control pills.

Four to a dorm, alone together
for the first time in a new town,
Rolling Stones blaring on the HiFi:
Hey, You, Get Off Of My Cloud.

My mother stands triumphant
on the edge of the bedframe, takes turns
waiting, bounces on the wool blanket
then jumps back to the concrete floor.

A few years later she'll play these records for us:
Each morning when Father leaves the house,
she'll bring her albums down, watching
her toddlers pore through those photos.

Inspired by the ancient teenagers,
we'll sway to *Rubber Soul* in the living room,
thinking the Beatles were her friends, too.
Their four faces stare at us in syncopated mystery,
we'll dance and pretend to know the words
until we learn the words, rehearse them over and over,

while she lives her story over and over until the clouds
she jumped off of dissipate and scatter—
cumulus, then nimbus, then gone.

Late Summer

Even in this city neighborhood cicadas hide in cracks
of sidewalks, behind telephone poles, emanating
reverberative melody, synonymous with summer.
I walk home from the subway stained in perspiration,
worry, my face breaks into agitated beads soothed only
by promise of ice cream, the Deli's avuncular neon sign.
Teenage boys stand on the corner, pants hanging in
saggy droops, shiny sports jerseys tucked just so,
a casual construction. Their hands move with eloquence,
gymnasts flipping cell phones and beepers, gesturing
at slow-passing cars. They are unspeakably beautiful.
Dusk covers them, covers me, covers the boulevard
until we are all washed through. Their little phones chirp
and buzz, fissures of overworked electricity starch the air,
echoes of basketballs' staccato dribbles coil up at edges of evening.
It's too much to want more than this minute, this singular reprieve.

Offering, Rio Grande

Put a plate of food
by the river, let the moon
do some work on rice,
chicken gravy necklaced
with peppers.

Maybe she will come,
he trims the tall grass
so he can see—puts down
miniature daisies and names them
(their children).

Her voice is the shaking
of imagined maracas:

No necesita nada mas.

—

Her head is
stamped on his forehead,
an icon, frowning.

Since he can't be with her
he talks to that head,
teaches it slow songs…

Cabesito, why don't you smile?

—

Hueso de la suerte—it's just a bone,
broken from a wish, taken
from the last turkey she cooked.

The bone is now ragged
with his pulling, the desire for her.

Isn't it funny,
this unlucky thing gets kept?

Enemies

San Juan, Puerto Rico

The women in line tell me about her rivals, gossip
about *las enemigas, diablas* who leave premeditated
messes in her stalls. Infamous for making clientele
wait, she is *la Doña*, high priestess in her public
restroom by the park—the backsplash of her sinks
are altars of aerosol, lip balm, maxi pads, antacids,
Kleenex, parfum. White and gray tiles coruscate
opalescence from her impromptu cleanings, routine
shuttings down for essential repairs. "It's hot out here!"
patrons complain, place addled hands between their legs
and beg again: "*Please*, let us in…"

I want to have enemies, hold up the line, hordes
of people outside pleading for consideration.
When it's my turn, I proffer the required 50 cents,
side-step luminaria stationed in corners, cross myself
before numinous toilet bowls and counter, the build-up
so sanctimonious, I forget to look in the mirror.
When I'm done, she gives me a final once-over,
snarls disapproval and brandishes her mop: a signal
to come forward, anoint my hands under her faucet.

Bluethroat

We—are the Birds—that stay.
                    —Emily Dickinson

I.

Old-world flycatcher building your nest of shreds,
thing with feathers, skeptic in wet birchwood,
bushy swamps. A bonanza of souvenirs lines your
eccentric retreat—bottle caps, coins, tissues, hair,
shoelaces, lint. Intense mystic shut in a sanctum
of twigs, grass, gum.

Your gorgeous, imitative voice—polyphony,
kibitzer of dense shrubs. Your neck reveals its inky
stain, up writing again, wily assembler of insects,
snippets of woodnote, moss.

II.

Emily dreams she's won the lottery,
a yellow ticket rests cockeyed on her desk.
She's still waiting to collect—the voracious
din of Amherst, little Bluethroat loitering
in her room, her habit, dovecote, penning
with a feather dipped in ink. Backlogged
fantasies, commemorations of reclusive
ecstasy—Yes, she's hit the jackpot,
sculptural dashes rubbernecking from windows
that line her roost. Selecting her society
of birds, amber, clover, honeyed flower.
Nature's mitzvahs, rejoice: *At Home—in Paradise.*

Late at Night, Knitting

It's easy to talk, and writing words on the page
doesn't involve much risk as a general rule:
you might as well be knitting late at night.

—Philippe Jaccottet

I am doing something useful with my hands,
in this room of full Odyssean light, knotting

cables with a fine-point pen, words and feathers,
ink blobs, sequined stitches to make literary

outfits, articulations of what I am unable to say.
This is my work, plaiting together vernacular

from dissonant strands, interlocking words
and passions, adding myself to the taratantara

of the world. A tired motif, I'm a Penelope
buying time, twined in a long series of purple loops

that sew and mesh my grief into a woolly silence.
Someday what I think will rise out of this apartment,

days of threading metaphor through the needle's
static eye. In the meantime, I won't unravel my handiwork.

All these booties, alliterative buntings, scarves,
sweaters of indignation and longing are meant to honor life,

written to speak, to knit, which is to connect.

Brooklyn Tropicale

Green birds give birth to themselves
out of the bottom of traffic lights
on Clinton Street, emerald sequiny

things, mangoes with wings—content,
I think, to perch in the boughs
of coconut oaks, folks passing by

with guavas in carriages, or babies,
dogs, more cooing from the roofs
of brick-housed blocks.

On the Promenade, tugboats
pump out a meringue beat.
Plaster Jesuses in plexiglass boxes

pose on Bergen, hands bloody
from prayer. "Hey there," I say
on my way to the subway station

where green tiles sparkle like lottery dollars.
I can't stop the tempo in my shoes—
on the platform, watching a G train go,

I belt out my notes, halos float
like traffic lights or smoke-rings
from unexpected cigars.

And the F will be along soon,
I'll hear it, a low-slung string of bungalows:
Feel dreamy, they'll sing, *feel really sweet.*

The Elephants

for Paige

enter Manhattan, feet plodding
toward a night opening with neon, huge
heads, reflective harnesses,
through the lip of the Midtown Tunnel.

We have seen them before,
these gray-skinned mammals,
wrinkled and swarthy,
moving left to right.

They are the men in our dreams, carrying us
inside wicker carriages across fields
with atmospheres so light we breathe
with our heads between our legs,

only coming up for seconds at a time to admire
blues and purples of the loose skin
we ride on. That long, flexible snout
wavering back to tickle

in our ears until
we hear our own sad mothers crying,
their ring fingers with diamonds
reflecting code in dashes of light.

But it is 2 a.m. and the elephants are scared,
cameras flash in their eyes, they walk past Macy's
down Sixth Avenue, trumpeting blank sounds.
Under our breath we tell them to hang on, to get some sleep.

We want to throw ourselves in front of them, paste
dumb prayers at the base of our throats, on the pavement
to Madison Square Garden, the circus, and those inevitable
beds of hay.

Mona Thinks of Crying

Some days it bothers her less—
lovers, the spaces
between bodies.

In front of her a couple
reaches to itself: fingers
excuse themselves to an arm,
the inclination of sides.

Smiles break across
their faces—herself,
snug between margins.

It's been building up
behind those oval eyes—so much
kept inside without merger
or breakfast—alone only
to know herself.

She is tired.
What would it be like for her hand
to meet her face? To blend
tears with canvas?

Inadequate, what could she do
if she had the chance? Made
from liquids she tries to fathom
returning there—so dry,
release seems impossible.

Mona Lisa and the Dragonfly

"Don't be sad," his wings crack and her back
shudders from sudden involvement.

"Don't cry," he whispers.
(A tear) he thinks he sees one,

octagonal, as he nests
in the black back of her hair.

Come near, she drones
but he is already
close.

She can't see him
but ascertains: *He's there.*

"I want you," the dragonfly barks back,
super-buzzed from her hair—

then disappears.

Lost One

The London ferris wheel has capsules,
empty pills in rotation like the ones I took
to keep you at bay. My children, my child,
were you carried there in the boxcars behind me?

Kicking my feet, rocking the seat back
for a more impressive ride, I was transfixed
by the throngs below, their delicate exhale
and inhale, a heartbeat. I ignored

Big Ben's twitching clicks as each second
switched forward into eternity. I was ridiculous,
fastidious not to repeat my mother's mistake,
I would not look back at you then.

Unborn visitors shifting into place one by one,
I never asked: *Will you choose me?* But you did,
on a windy afternoon, stopped on top, wavering
so long, for so long—then you disappeared.

The Unisphere

I.
My mother is a teen upstate, learning
about boys in a small town, how to hold
herself so people won't notice the woman inside.
Even though Jack Kennedy promised her
a man on the moon by decade's end,

she will not go to see the debut of color TV,
The Happy Plastic Family or touch-tone phones,
no *Better Living Through Chemistry*,
no pavilions hawking the futurama that awaits.

I am unborn—1964, the Unisphere
is twelve stories of stainless steel,
tilted model of the earth, 700,000-pound
wedding diamond upended on three prongs
for the World's Fair.

My mother will not see the view from the edge
of the reflecting pool. In these few years before
she is pregnant, she will not know the world
as it appears 6,000 miles in space. She can't

even guess at the pressure building up inside
the structure because the Earth's land masses
aren't evenly distributed. Curved sheets of steel lift
and bend during heavy winds, threatening onlookers below.

Later, in her hometown, my mother turns and runs
from her own pressures, stops in place outside
the back-alley's door because it is dirty and shameful
and no one will help her.

In a matter of seconds, her world shrinks.

II.
I was not even an inkling, as the three rings
were built representing man-made satellites,
orbiters of the world where I live now.
The Unisphere, tattered icon in the park behind my apartment,
illuminated ornament of outdated promise, world dominance
come to pass. My president says: *Bring It On*, children kick

soccer balls, navigate remote-control cars, ride skateboards
and rollerblades at the base. Their young parents worry
about safety, no remnants of those two World's Fair

summers gleaming in the blacktop's mica, when companies
celebrated *Man's Achievements on a Shrinking Globe*,
most now obsolete. At dusk, tracers of clouds arc

in the sun, planes take off and land too close; birds settle
on tension wires. Dust swirls, stars implode in spite of themselves.
I walk in the empty fountain with graffiti, soda cans and leaves.

Used-up cigarettes gather in puddles, I study the reflection as
a stench of sulfur looms: raised land masses, slices of steel
molded into features on a precarious, disfigured face.

One girl drops her scooter on the fountain's faded blue floor,
Paraté, she screams at her mother, *Stop!* She's not ready to go home.

Mona's Box

A crystal case constructed to protect
from angry crowds, men who stab?

The tourists'
cameras flash in penitent codes,

waiting, watching
bright angles reflected back.

To be a gemstone:
opening and opening...

doubled-over dots of brilliance,

all dazzling, all inside.

Untangling Jewelry

Almost sundown at the racetrack flea market, I dip my hands into
the velvet-lined box of jewels, rhinestones gleam in multi-colors.

I'm ten, I've found a way to be alone while others pack away
teacups and Depression glass, dismantle furniture.

I stand with my box, straighten old ladies' necklaces and bracelets
beaded with imitation crystals, plastic, wood.

I have patience to let my fingers follow tangles to their source,
unlock twisted chains and hooks lodged into metal loops.

Slow and deliberate, I lift each link away and out of its snarl.
Hour after hour, I think of boys who might love me

when I am older and finally beautiful. The pins and chokers,
spangled gems which belonged to my mother's mother—

a murky outline, her glasses had rhinestones, twinkled facets
at the corner of each eye.

She left me a ring, heart-shaped, turquoise meeting
red in blurry edges at the middle.

But I want *my* mother. I want to reach her, undo
the ache knotted inside our bodies.

Dust sparkles emanate from under her bedroom door—
her body buried in those pillows, a diamond refusing to be set.

Prisoner

She has only her pillow
to lean on. Her mute body
vanishes beneath a white
gown, what might blaze
from her memory is limitless—
what can stay hidden
will remain so forever.

She won't speak
and becomes nameless,
answering in silence
when her hands reach,
their touch twitters and falls
like the birds outside.

The taunting, alive birds,
they cover the windows
and melt into the walls.

Her bedclothes unravel and
toss themselves onto the floor.
At any moment, she will disintegrate—
a thin dust, a film of dreaming

in her own home.

String of Pearls

Moonglow giggles on the windows around them, teenagers,
young wives loosey-goosey on a train. They head south

to The Big Apple, their lodestar channeling luster, layers
of calcium carbonate deposited far from their farms.

This was her favorite story, newly married, before children,
the late nineteen thirties strung out and swinging in standbys,

a clarinet sweet and lowdown. My grandmother plays
with her liberty at the Pennsylvania Hotel—wiggle and stomp,

One O'Clock Jump, live orchestra with the King of Swing,
son of Russia, full of rhythm for his Scots-Irish girl.

Her own good man waits at home, stringing beans and wheat
and corn seeds into the ground. Pomp and romance,

big bands and bigger plans, nothing can stop her, champagne
and yellow roses at midnight, special delivery, a telegram

from the farm: *Happy Birthday*, stop. I love you, stop.
The girls Lindy Hop in a radiant ballroom full of balloons,

streamers hover in tangles at the corners of chandeliers.
Lillian touches luxury she later dreams about, before children,

before the slow fizz of years. She purses her lips at a gold
powder case, her fingers deliberate in their dash, a circlet of red—

out all night—the mob of martinis, these lovely, giddy ladies jump
back on an early train, the only time they ever go to New York,

celebrating their friend, newly married, turning twenty or was it nineteen?
The beautiful irritation of years calcified into nostalgia, now gone.

Train windows blaze with the rising sun, the tractors' clamor
echoes in the din of wheels, whistles and bells.

All Aboard!, girls switching seats and laughing, evergreen.

The Combine

I.

As wheat came through the thresher, chaff flew.
My grandfather drove and my father or uncle followed
with the baler, pitching finished bales off the side.
Ernest from up the hill lost his whole hand
in his combine. Sitting on back, I'd watch
the field mice and rabbits get caught in the blades,
end up later, packed neatly into a block of hay.
At six, I knew there was no place to go
once the blade hits you—except to get
bundled in with grass, dirt, straw.

Bolting through the field barelegged each day,
I sliced up my calves and knees,
freshly cut wheat sharp
as an attacker's pocket knife.
No amount of grandma's ointment
or whiskey or love could help.
I'd be out there again the next day,
with the other animals—
dancing and darting, tempting
the combine's thick edge.

II.

Just taller than the wheat,
I waited for something to happen—
breaktime or cows to burst over the fence,
men stammering in off their tractors, their girlfriends
left sighing momentarily in the fields.

On grandmother's lawn we served them: piles
of bread and sausages held in grit-caked hands.
My hands shook, poured water over ice in their glasses,
a flurry of chewing. Leftover hulls from the threshers bounced
out of their sleeves, work clothes soiled with chaff. No talk.

III.
In the kitchen, grandmother dreamed of ocean liners.
Waltzing with her grace undisguised, she soared and panted,
the pantry gleamed in her smile. I held a washed plate at my chest
like a moon, a life-preserver, gangplanks and portholes
got imagined to the music box: *Hi Lili, hi Lili, hi Lo...*

When the handle came unwound I'd twirl it again for her,
I'd glide around after her—Lily, her own name, her body

reeling into dizzy sparks.

III.

Scat Mona, Scat!

It overcomes her
and somebody whispers

"Ella." The Lisa,

unable to croon, careens
in her mind, her inescapable

situation—the tourists
(who's got the radio?),

a guard rushes over.

Mona: *A biddilydibbitybidditty get me out of here, bop!*

Mona Rides

She tries to picture herself
as not a picture,

riding in an automobile
(though she can hardly imagine).

She's seen the women who come here.
She's not them.

They are flush and she,
flat: indistinguishable,
her hair from her dress
from the background from the wall.

She can't laugh.

Humor, her strategy,
won't keep these thoughts away.

In that automobile, her hair—how
she'd unfold inside if it was blowing.

If, by some miracle, the wind
would take it and lift
from the roots—

elastic, smooth.

Oh sweetness, alive—
in the air then blown forward,
wrapping her face.

Autogenic

The expressway's shoulders hold no promise,
driving home, bound to road, purple asters
bloom in the median—late summer, time
for harvest, release. The last of light evenings
breaks through full, humid air. I cling to cheer,
a poetic surface dilates and expectations linger
for more warm, long days. But darkness always tailgates,
moving forward through sunset's hazy debris.
One truck has loosed a whole shipment of film, celluloid
ribbons flicker, tossed all over, they glisten and flutter
past windows as commuters point themselves home.
It's our lives as a movie pouring out in thousands of stills,
glossy trajectories recombine into alternate endings.
An uncanny soundtrack blares—autogenic, I process
my own music: of trees and bushes, asters and
fireflies thickening to intermittent flares.

A Dentist's Lament

Day of The Dead, Brooklyn

Inside his car, an '83 Toyota,
He performs what's necessary:
the children's back molars get
especially dirty. They recline
in the front seat as he sits behind
them to examine. Some wait
on the sidewalk outside for his care,

fussing with leftover lollipops,
climbing all over the hood.
Fish lights from Woolworth's
decorate his windshield,
plugged into the lighter, maybe
pulse later, in a five-year-old's
sleep—while he can do no more

than a ritual cleaning, get the plaque,
trash, *basura*, and hand out free floss.
He does not pretend for a minute
that it helps, but the fish-lights
go on, and he remembers *La Virgen*,
smiling down at his tools,
his mirrors and hand-picks

and knows it's November,
pumpkins overturned
like skulls in the street, cavities
worsened from Halloween.

If there are souls out here today,
he says: *Let me get visited,*
let me ask them if their work is done.

Avec Kafka

New Jewish Cemetery, June 3

I searched all secondhand Prague for you,
Prosím, moving through overcast silence, *XXX* and
erotica shops—the city's scarlet and cream towers,
markers of how to bring myself back. *Kavka*,
cousin to the jackdaw, *corvus manedula*, nesting
in the cavities of trees or graves. At your grave,
alone, I wait out the anniversary—moss-stained
obelisks, ivy-covered mounds sloping to the East.
Birds jargon in their scraps of speech, crude angels
prognosticating rain. Cars whoosh by like the ocean,
your resting place a bed of stones left by pilgrim
wanderers, still warm and worn from touching.

Going to Laredo

Finally, enough dry air
to soak me up—brush and tumbleweed
and the word *fiesta*.

No yield signs, no caution,
a red Cadillac
with license plate: ON FIRE.

The Rio Grande is somewhere
around here, cow skulls and cans
pile at the side of the road.

It's an instruction tape,
the secret to living:
Eat sensible, talk slow,

don't throw yourself on a cactus
no matter how confused your desire.

Magnolias, Poolside

There is no telling how exotic I am tonight
by the pool at the Lawton Ramada—soldiers,
young men from Fort Sill run in and out
of their rooms looking for more beer
and company. It is midnight and my long
hair is wet. I soak in the full moon
through magnolia trees, cedar trees
reflected in the water. The soldiers
look at me from their hotel room windows,
a woman staring into the pool. Some of them
exchange stories about who I could be.
The light on the pool becomes a mirror,
damp sick smell of magnolias.
I decide that pain is a relative,
a heaviness to be counted on. Crash!
A bottle? One of the soldiers comes over
and asks: *Want to join our party?*
He explains there are four guys and only
three girls and wouldn't I like to watch a movie?
When the answer comes, he does not expect it.
It startles him, a woman as young as he is
alone, by the pool.

Rest Stop, Adrian TX

I like it here—my waitress chews
gum better than anyone, I watch the pellet
cha-ching from cheek to cheek.
It is brighter than Sunday
in this diner, flies take five
on the table then buzz off.
It's a movie, a foreign film
and I make up the subtitles.
The waitress, nameless,
brings potatoes—outside trees slide
sideways, Route 66 goes on...
I watch the teenaged busboy
grow a beard, his first,
isolated hairs help him resemble
a catfish—Henri, I call him—he brings
water and more water, like a favorite scene
from another movie where the heroine,
unsatisfied, runs outside to the rain—
bawling, she asks for a glass
of water, only to be made more unhappy
when it comes. My waitress asks
where I'm from—*Not Texas*, she says,
takes back the plate, hesitates,
her hands on the sides of her hips as if I'd tell her my life.
Does blah come from blasé
or blasphemy?
The busboy balances water glasses
on his tray—he brings them over
so I can send them back.

Parrot Stand

Towards the airport, on the highway,
with lanes that encourage drifting,
we drive and talk and the horizon wavers
behind our green car—a warmed bubble
of chatting, glances and shy smiles.
Time ticks in jazz licks, half-witted us, dumbed
by conversation we've missed our exit, don't know
where we are anymore.

Still, there are people to ask, a man hawking
chili-peppers and Texana from the back of his car—
a straw ten-gallon hat on his head orbits and flirts.
Dust clouds our eyes as we hold hands and cross
the way for a second opinion. You throw a chili-pepper
wreath on your shoulder and we move over to the next
roadside stand where another man, selling parrots,
points his hands and appears to be giving directions.

I nod as if listening but I am long gone, green
and yellow birds adjust themselves on top of perches.
I stare at the chilies wrapped hot over your chest,
X-mas bulbs out of season, pulsing as you return
pleasantries with the parrot-man. I can't stand that
you must go again, yet I poise myself in acceptance.
As we get back in the car, the parrots belt out
some dissonant squawks, arias for loved-ones
who live apart.

Near Uvalde, TX

Cattle stand at the side
of the road and stare at me,

clumps of cacti and short
tough trees.

Oil derricks bend over
as I pass (the idea of it)

orange dust
and a hymn about loneliness.

Nothing to be inspired by but road,
and this promise: Keep going.

At the rest stop two kids set up shop
in a Cadillac—steam from a steel

bucket in the front seat, the human smell
of tomatoes. *¿Quieres tamales?*

they ask, tuned-in
to my hunger.

I tell them no, an ice-cream truck
passes—

the air is both flat and prickly.

Tijuana and South

In Mexico, we watch mementos near the road, *recuerdos* of whole
families killed by a crash. Homespun altars, flowers and glass

glued to crosses that won't bring back the dead, but warn others now
to be careful, and please, on your life, go slow.

Outside *Guerrero Negro* it is midnight and we're driving
through heavy rain, only the tough heads of cacti dare show themselves

in our headlights. There is hardly another motorist to break up the night,
our car evolves into a kind of submarine, negotiating

this desert Atlantis until a man and a dog appear in the road,
flagging us down. We almost hit them, but swerve, pull our car over

to the side of a cliff where a crowd mills around.
I ask myself: What's brought these people out?,

and feel instantly afraid. They might be *los banditos* the guidebooks
describe, the reason no one is supposed to travel past dark.

A woman comes to my side. In Spanish, she says
there has been a crash, an accident with schoolchildren in a bus

totaling another, smaller car. She cries nervously that authorities
haven't come to remove the bodies, that the opening between vehicles

is too tight a space to pass. I look over the mountains and expect
to see them ascending one by one,

but catch only a tattered glimpse of stars. A young boy
approaches us—I convince myself he is *your* ghost.

My bones jump as he motions to me. I think he is going to say
the accident is our accident, that we are dead, that our life together is over.

Instead, he says he's been to the wreck, thinks our car is small enough
to get through, that we should try to make it and find help.

I don't want to translate, to push on, I am afraid I'll see only
the broken bodies of children, *angelcitos*, for the rest of my life.

Jean Claude and Christo's *The Gates*

Central Park, Valentine's Day

Dusk: We enter from Harlem, the *AltaGracía* Deli a beacon
near 116th and Fifth. Airplanes tear scraps of heaven from clouds—
blue chalk, aquamarine, paler blue. Security lights flash
up and down the hill. Later, we'll feed each other slippery mussels
fresh from the market. We stroll with other couples framed in saffron;
holding your hand, silhouettes of trees emerge against an almost night sky.
We move from Meer to North Meadow, the wind picks up
and The Gates are nightshirts saturated with love, Buddhist robes,
blooms on the line, live haiku by the thousands: lucky poems
incorporated into the landscape, this moment.

Buildings across the meadow sport tangerine skirts, illumination
arrives in antique lampposts while a helicopter swoons. Taking in
everything at once, for once, in the path of a silver-white moon.
Skirts and shower curtains, trash bags, laundry, hot coals from ancient fires,
flags sent as hopeful messages. The Gates look forward and wave back—
quiet looms as red hands flash danger in the crosswalks, the way things
settle in and go unnoticed. Refracted ginger permeates evening over the
Meer like a school of overfed koi swimming through February's
ice and mud, the Fauve orange I saw so long ago—at the Metropolitan,
in portraits of distant villages with calm water and empty boats.

Look how far they've come to greet us, to say: *You are part of the landscape too.*

City Lions

We are sitting *flâneurs* by the fountain in Bryant Park,
amid pink impatiens in planters fashioned to buxom minarets.
Yes, we are *bon vivants* readying as the sun lowers to set,
library patrons jostle and mill through the spray, sparrows
flitter through trees in search of better seats.

It is too warm, in November, lamp poles overdressed
with garnet ribbons and fir, this season out of season.
Tourists, polyglottish, take snapshots, serenades pipe
from a makeshift skating rink.

People blab into their cell phones as a Zamboni
glides past—blurred speech becomes another background,
taxonomies of folks eating pizza and treats, children's squeals,
poodles on pompommed legs, workers carry projects spooled
into scrolls, pigeons nudging trash with mechanized beaks.

The city's twinkle lights materialize: white and amber, amethyst,
a soloist pines with some indiscriminate ache. The moon
peeks out over the Chrysler Building, sliced perfectly in half,
it gazes back to the fountain as skaters migrate in circles
around their icy blue jewelbox, our twilight.

Dervishes

At the post office, they spend too long at the window,
asking about stamps, postage, how many make up
the extra ounce? Other line dwellers grow restless,
one man complains, *People have stuff to do,* as
a mismatched woman regales the clerk with stories
of kismet and envelopes stockpiled at home. Stamps shift
on her fingertips like cubist butterflies—*Some of them
are older than me,* she quips, her socks crumpled, loose,
hanging over her shoes. Faded caps and tattered wool coats,
the lonelyhearts shuffle from spot to spot all over the city,
carrying their lotus bowls at diner counters, laundromats, banks.
They hold up lines and kvetch or sigh, something always compared
to how it used to be, a summary of bliss. Mystics deposited
in public restrooms, drugstores, turnstiles. They twirl and mutter,
sputter: every reception area, an invocation.

Housebird Suite

I.
Sheets of sound surround my one-bedroom—
arguments, arpeggios flow up from the floorboards,
radios, vacuum cleaners, outside the tearing
down and building of more apartments, aviaries.
Power tools hammer in their syntax of progress,
our lush lives vocalized, streaming audio in conventional
rounds of fifths, old tonal variations repeating the same
motifs: *to live, to dwell.* My starlings, sparrows,
familiar virtuosos, how much we are at home together.

II.
Trying to play out what I hear in my head,
I feel played. Happy coos from the adjoining
walls, a woman with babies—all day the feed and cry,
piquant diablerie, peals of glee, new birds bustle
while I'm in a soulful mood. Tails and wingfeathers
well groomed, thriving on guttural riffs, their
throats holler: *Be bop, so easy to love.*

So easy to love, flanked by diapers and chirping toys,
my own nest is vacant, reverberates blank chords.

III.
When the ambulance comes, we are witnesses
and we judge—on the sidewalk, stammering
canaries gather and circle, hushed but still
hovering by bushes, we pray and repent.

The sheriff's amber light flashes through curtains,
sending signals that someone is hurt, or dead.
We peep out our windows to the street, half-hoping
to glimpse what we do not want to see.

We can barely move without impacting each other,
our stoicism speaks for itself.

On Park Row by the Brooklyn Bridge

A dump truck with bold letters, FORTUNE,
waits for me, idling at the curb as I sit inside
a coffee shop downtown, staring at the Woolworth's
Bldg, World Trade Center gone, paper Xmas
wreaths oscillate in the window.

Could I breathe in the world's suffering?
Just for one second, make room. Passersby
chatter to themselves, a quartet waits at the corner,
grown men holding suitcases and holiday bags,
DOT trucks zoom past with brooms and helium.

I feel light: So many experiences left to have!
Yellow buses and red buses, double-deckers with
tourists seeking their sights; how cheery they are.
Babies and nannies, taxis, outrageous SUVs.
Suddenly in the chill of early December, I forget to grieve.

After Hours

...a moderate amount of smoke produces the finest blue.
—Leonardo da Vinci, *Notebooks*

Late at night they come crawling round—azure,
cerulean, cobalt hues.

Periwinkle, midnight patterned on floors.
She's paid her dues, this Mona—MOMA Mama,

the blues are just a carpet her feet
are resting on—ultramarine, teal.

She thinks the lady don't protest enough.
Move it, Louvre, get into the motion

of your mission, lonely nightclub
with hallways full of loot.

Wouldn't a cigarette taste good?
Exhale a little?

Sprinklers or no—
something's got to give.

Wonder Wheel

August 2001

Our art is here, revolving in satellites inconceivable
to us, like the red and white cars swirling on top
of Coney Island's Wonder Wheel, built in 1920
out of steel girders from Bethlehem—*never an accident,*
braggadocio or no, our own transmissions keep turning
in prayer wheels or atoms attached invisible inside ankles,
collarbones, fleshy hindquarters holding dreams written
in codes on scrap paper, spun into cylindrical dervishes
that orbit and enchant our lives unfolding mythic narratives
of trees and kisses, starlight swimming in convolutions of hair.

To the right—Manhattan, World Trade Towers sway toward
each other, a tuning fork lending its tone to the muggy summer
4/4 time. The Verrazano Bridge is loops and loops of tape.
Leftover rides from Steeplechase Park flow lonely in the haze,
an old roller coaster covered with vegetation, catalyzed into
a mountainous topiary. It tickles the foot of the Parachute Drop
with its many-leveled, herbaceous tongue. All of these sing,
these *things*, simultaneously within us and out.

The waters of the Atlantic sparkle at the brim, lulling the pier.
Children run with plastic cups, birds flying, the smell of fish,
French fries, hot dogs, corn and mangoes on sticks, flags with white
stars floating in the middle, mermaids and sea creatures drink *cervezas*
to a marimba beat. *Por Fin*—finally, at last—wavers from a square
radio while fishermen lean back all the way in their chairs,
their lines are already cast.

The book was designed by Lesley Landis Designs.

Printed in the USA
CPSIA information can be obtained
at www.ICGtesting.com
JSHW052020140824
68134JS00027B/2559